Paws
AND
Claws

SLOTHS

Sara Swan Miller

PowerKiDS
press.

New York

For Danny and Amelia,
who are anything but slothful

Published in 2008 by The Rosen Publishing Group, Inc.
29 East 21st Street, New York, NY 10010

First Edition

Editor: Amelie von Zumbusch
Book Design: Julio Gil
Photo Researcher: Nicole Pristash

Photo Credits: Cover © Michael & Patricia Fogden/Getty Images; pp. 5, 9, 11, 17, 21 Shutterstock.com; p. 7 © istockphoto.com/Matt Coats; p. 13 © istockphoto.com/Derek Dammann; p. 15 © istockphoto.com/Patrick Sinke; p. 19 © SuperStock, Inc.

Library of Congress Cataloging-in-Publication Data

Miller, Sara Swan.
  Sloths / Sara Swan Miller.
      p. cm. — (Paws and claws)
  Includes index.
  ISBN 978-1-4042-4166-4 (library binding)
  1. Sloths—Juvenile literature. I. Title.
  QL737.E2M55 2008
  599.3'13—dc22
                                                        2007025884

Manufactured in the United States of America

Contents

The World's Slowest Mammals

Sloths are slow-moving **mammals** that spend most of their life hanging upside down in the trees. They are the slowest mammals in the world. They could never outrun their enemies. Sloths cannot run at all!

There are six known **species** of sloths. All these sloths are part of an order, or group, called **Xenarthra**. The other animals in this group are the pointy-nosed armadillos and anteaters. Sloths do not look much like these animals. However, sloths, armadillos, and anteaters all have extra strong backbones and no front teeth.

If you look closely at this slow-moving sloth, you can see a baby sloth on its stomach!

Where Do Sloths Live?

Sloths live only in parts of Central America and South America. They hang high in the trees in the warm, wet **rain forests**. Sloths have a very low body **temperature**. They cannot stand the cold. When the Sun is out, they climb higher in the trees and warm themselves in the sunlight.

In the wet rain forest, water is almost always dripping from a sloth's long brown fur. Green **algae** often grow all over a sloth's wet body. This makes a sloth hard to see against the leaves. Even if a sloth were right above you, you still might not spot it.

Sloths spend most of their time in the canopies, or high branches, of their rain-forest homes.

Two Toes or Three?

There are two types of sloths. Three-toed sloths have three toes on each of their feet. A two-toed sloth has three toes on its back feet but only two toes on its front feet. Two-toed sloths have fewer neck bones than three-toed sloths do, so their neck is shorter. Three-toed sloths have a short tail, but two-toed sloths have no tail. Two-toed sloths are generally bigger and heavier than three-toed sloths.

Aside from these differences, both kinds of sloths look and act very much the same. They pull their hairy body from branch to branch as they search for food.

Southern two-toed sloths, like this one, live in South America.
They are also known as Linnaeus' two-toed sloths.

What Do Sloths Look Like?

Sloths have a small, round head with short ears hidden under their fur. They do not hear well, but their big brown eyes can see very well. Sloths also have a very good sense of smell. Their little black nose helps them smell out their favorite foods.

Sloths have a coat of short, warm underfur. They are covered with long brown hair. Their fur grows differently from other animals' fur. Instead of growing from the back down to the legs, their fur grows from the stomach down to the back. This makes sense because sloths spend their life upside down.

Most sloths are about 2 feet (61 cm) long, from their nose to their tail.
This is a bit smaller than a Labrador retriever.

Long, Long Claws

Sloths have very long claws. These claws may be 4 inches (10 cm) long. Sloths use their curved, or curled, claws to hang from branches. Their **grip** is very strong. Even after a sloth dies, it will keep hanging from its branch. Many hunters know this. They do not bother to shoot sloths because sloths are so hard to pull from the treetops.

On the ground, a sloth is nearly helpless. Its legs are weak, and its claws get in the way. To move, a sloth must lie on its stomach, hold on to tree roots, and pull itself slowly along the ground.

A sloth's long claws curve. This makes it easier for the sloth to hold on to round branches.

13

Life in the Trees

Sloths spend most of their life hanging in the trees. Mostly, they sleep. Sloths sleep between 15 and 18 hours a day. They like to sleep in **coconut palms**, where they look like large coconuts. Sloths generally wake up at night. Hand over hand, they make their way ever so slowly from branch to branch. Sloths generally move no faster than 1 foot (30 cm) a minute. A sloth will never get arrested for going too fast!

Once in a while, a sloth may fall out of its tree and into the water. Luckily, sloths are good swimmers.

Sloths live in several kinds of rain-forest trees. Many sloths live in cecropia trees. These tall trees have groups of big leaves.

Baby Sloths

Mother sloths even give birth in the trees, hanging upside down. A sloth generally has just one baby a year. The tiny baby weighs only ½ pound (227 g). It climbs up onto its mother's stomach and hangs on to her fur. The mother nurses her baby with her milk for about six weeks. Then the baby starts reaching for adult food, while still hanging on to its mother's fur.

When the baby is nine months old, its mother drives it away. The baby has to go find its own trees in which to live.

This sloth baby is hanging on tightly to its mother. Sloth babies are good at holding on to things.

Hungry Sloths

When a sloth is not sleeping, it is generally eating. A sloth eats mostly leaves and buds. Sloths feed on 30 different kinds of trees. They have no front teeth for nipping off leaves. Instead, they wrap their tongue around the leaves and yank them off. Then the sloths chew the leaves with their back teeth.

Sloths have a large stomach. A third of a sloth's weight is the food in its stomach. A sloth **digests** its food very slowly. It can take a month for a sloth's food to travel through its stomach!

Sloths do everything, including eating, slowly. They take a long time to chew their food.

Danger!

There are plenty of animals that have a taste for sloths. Birds called harpy eagles strike from the sky. Large snakes may swallow sloths whole. On the ground, a sloth has to look out for ocelots and jaguars, two large cats with powerful claws and sharp teeth. The best **protection** a sloth has is staying still and being hard to see in the trees. Most **predators** do not even notice sloths.

If a sloth does get cornered, it strikes out with its long, sharp claws. Sometimes that is enough to drive an enemy away. A sloth's heavy coat also helps protect it.

Predators, such as this jaguar, do not often notice sloths in the treetops. However, jaguars sometimes catch sloths that have come down to the ground.

21

Sloths Throughout History

Long ago, during the **Ice Age**, another kind of sloth lived in South America and North America. It was the giant ground sloth. This sloth grew to the size of an elephant. Unlike today's sloths, the giant ground sloth lived on the ground. It likely walked on its back legs. When people came to South America and North America, they hunted the giant sloths. Now these sloths are **extinct**.

Even two-toed sloths and three-toed sloths are less common than they once were. People have been cutting down their rain-forest homes. However, people are now trying to protect the rain forests and the gentle sloths.

Glossary

algae (AL-jee) Plantlike living things without roots or stems.

coconut palms (KOH-kuh-nut POMZ) Trees that grow in warm places and bear fruits with hard, brown outsides and soft, white insides, called coconuts.

digests (dy-JESTS) Breaks down food so that the body can use it.

extinct (ek-STINKT) No longer living.

grip (GRIP) A firm hold.

Ice Age (YS AYJ) A period of time about 12,000 years ago.

mammals (MA-mulz) Warm-blooded animals that have backbones and hair, breathe air, and feed milk to their young.

predators (PREH-duh-terz) Animals that kill other animals for food.

protection (pruh-TEK-shun) Something that keeps something else from being hurt.

rain forests (RAYN FOR-ests) Thick forests that receive a large amount of rain during the year.

species (SPEE-sheez) One kind of living thing. All people are one species.

temperature (TEM-pur-cher) How hot or cold something is.

Xenarthra (ZEN-ahr-thruh) A group of animals that includes armadillos, anteaters, and sloths.

Index

A
algae, 6
anteaters, 4
armadillos, 4

C
Central America, 4
claws, 12, 20
coconut palms, 14

F
fur, 6, 10, 16

J
jaguars, 20

M
mammals, 4

N
North America, 22

O
ocelots, 20

P
predators, 20

R
rain forest(s), 6, 22

S
snakes, 20
South America, 4, 22
stomach, 10, 12, 16, 18

T
teeth, 4, 18, 20
toes, 8

U
underfur, 10

X
Xenarthra, 4

Web Sites

Due to the changing nature of Internet links, PowerKids Press has developed an online list of Web sites related to the subject of this book. This site is updated regularly. Please use this link to access the list:
www.powerkidslinks.com/paws/sloths/